Meccano, ex parte U.S. Supreme Court
Transcript of Record with Supporting Pleadings

REEVE LEWIS

Meccano, ex parte
Petition / REEVE LEWIS / 1918 / 249 U.S. 594 / 39 S.Ct. 390 / 63 L.Ed. 793 / 10-1-1918

Meccano, ex parte U.S. Supreme Court
Transcript of Record with Supporting Pleadings

Table of Contents

Supreme Court of the United States

OCTOBER TERM, 1918.

No.   Original.   *481*

IN THE MATTER OF THE APPLICATION OF MEC-CANO LIMITED FOR A WRIT OF MANDAMUS, OR, IN THE ALTERNATIVE, FOR A WRIT OF PROHIBITION, DIRECTED TO THE UNITED STATES CIRCUIT COURT OF APPEALS FOR THE SECOND CIRCUIT, AND THE JUDGES THEREOF, AND TO THE UNITED STATES DISTRICT COURT FOR THE SOUTHERN DISTRICT OF NEW YORK, AND THE JUDGES THEREOF.

PETITION FOR WRIT OF MANDAMUS, OR FOR WRIT OF PROHIBITION,
and
BRIEF IN SUPPORT OF PETITION.

REEVE LEWIS,
C. A. L. MASSIE,
W. B. KERKAM,
RALPH L. SCOTT,
Counsel for Petitioner.

PRESS OF BYRON S. ADAMS, WASHINGTON, D. C.

Supreme Court of the United States

OCTOBER TERM, 1918.

No   , Original.

IN THE MATTER OF THE APPLICATION OF MEC-
CANO LIMITED FOR A WRIT OF MANDAMUS,
OR, IN THE ALTERNATIVE, FOR A WRIT OF
PROHIBITION, DIRECTED TO THE UNITED
STATES CIRCUIT COURT OF APPEALS FOR
THE SECOND CIRCUIT, AND THE JUDGES
THEREOF, AND TO THE UNITED STATES
DISTRICT COURT FOR THE SOUTHERN DIS-
TRICT OF NEW YORK, AND THE JUDGES
THEREOF.

MOTION.

Now comes the petitioner, MECCANO LIMITED, a
British corporation, by its counsel, and respectfully moves
this Honorable Court as follows:

(a) For leave to file the annexed petition for Writ of
Mandamus, or, in the alternative, for Writ of Prohibition;

(b) That a rule be entered and issued directing the Re-
spondents named in said petition to show cause why Writ
of Mandamus, or, in the alternative, Writ of Prohibition,
should not issue against them, and each of them, in accord-
ance with the prayers of said petition; and why said Petitioner should not have such other and further relief in the
premises as may be just and meet.

Dated May 1st, 1919.

/   REEVE LEWIS,
Of Counsel for Petitioner.

700 Tenth Street, N. W., Washington, D. C.

UNITED STATES SUPREME COURT.

OCTOBER TERM, 1918.

No: , Original.

IN THE MATTER OF THE APPLICATION OF MECCANO LIMITED FOR A WRIT OF MANDAMUS. OR, IN THE ALTERNATIVE, FOR A WRIT OF PROHIBITION, DIRECTED TO THE UNITED STATES CIRCUIT COURT OF APPEALS FOR THE SECOND CIRCUIT, AND THE JUDGES THEREOF, AND TO THE UNITED STATES DISTRICT COURT FOR THE SOUTHERN DISTRICT OF NEW YORK, AND THE JUDGES THEREOF.

PETITION FOR WRIT OF MANDAMUS, OR FOR WRIT OF PROHIBITION.

To the Honorable the Chief Justice and the Associate Justices of the Supreme Court of the United States:

This is a petition for Writ of Mandamus, or, in the alternative, for Writ of Prohibition, to stay the trial and all other proceedings in the cause of Meccano Limited vs. John Wanamaker, Equity 15/38, now pending in the Respondent District Court.

Your Petitioner, MECCANO LIMITED, a British corporation, complains:

(1) Of the errors in the order (printed in the margin)*
of the Respondent District Court, peremptorily setting down
for trial the aforesaid equity suit, entitled Meccano Limited
vs. John Wanamaker, New York, in Equity No. 15/38
(hereinafter referred to as the "Second Wanamaker Suit"),
and denying Petitioner's motion to say such trial until after
disposition by this Court of certain certiorari proceedings
now pending here as No. 614, October Term, 1918, and
arising out of an earlier and companion suit in said District
Court, between the same parties, entitled Meccano Limited
vs. John Wanamaker, New York, Equity No. 14/43 (and
hereinafter referred to as the "First Wanamaker Suit").

Your Petitioner has been informed, within the past few
days, that the Second Wanamaker Suit (here sought to be
stayed) is the thirteenth case assigned for trial at an Equity
Session of the Respondent District Court, to begin Monday, May 5th, 1919.

(2) Further complains of the errors in the order of the
Respondent Court of Appeals in dismissing Petitioner's
appeal (under Sec. 129 of the Judicial Code) from said
order of the Respondent District Court refusing to stay

---

* Plaintiff having noticed a motion for an order postponing the trial
of this case until after the disposition by the Supreme Court of the
United States of the companion suit previously instituted in this Court
(Equity No. 14/43) between the same parties hereto;

And said motion having come on to be heard upon the 22d day of
January, 1919, and counsel for the respective parties having been heard
and due consideration being had,

IT IS HEREBY ORDERED:

1. That the said motion of the plaintiff be and the same hereby is
in all respects denied; and

2. That the cause be set down peremptorily for hearing upon the
March, 1919, calendar of this Court.

(Signed) MANTON,
U. S. Circuit Judge.

Dated New York, N. Y., Feb. 6, 1919.

NO OBJECTION TO FORM, BUT EXCEPTION NOTED TO
RULING.

RALPH L. SCOTT,
Counsel for Plaintiff.

(enjoin) the trial of said Second Wanamaker Suit, said order reading:

> "A motion having been made herein by counsel for the appellee to dismiss the appeal herein upon the ground that this court has no jurisdiction to entertain the same;
> Upon consideration thereof it is
> ORDERED that said appeal be and hereby is dismissed.
> FURTHER ORDERED that a Mandate issue accordingly." (Filed April 17, 1919.)

(3) Further complains of the errors in the order of the Respondent Court of Appeals in denying Petitioner's petition for writ of mandamus, or for writ of prohibition, or for writ of certiorari, to stay said Second Wanamaker Suit until disposition by this Court of the aforesaid certiorari proceedings in said First Wanamaker Suit, said order reading:

> "A motion having been made herein by counsel for Meccano Limited for a writ of prohibition or mandamus directed to the Judges of the District Court of the United States for the Southern District of New York;
> Upon consideration thereof it is
> ORDERED that said motion be and hereby is denied." (Filed April 17, 1919.)

Petitioner respectfully shows:

I.

In both the aforesaid suits the Defendant, Wanamaker, is charged with unfair competition by its dealings in toy products charged to unlawfully imitate your Petitioner's toy product known as "Meccano."

The bill of complaint in said First Wanamaker Suit makes specific reference only to said Wanamaker's dealings in the so-called "American Model Builder" toy product manufactured by Francis A. Wagner, of Dayton, Ohio.

The bill of complaint in said Second Wanamaker Suit (in which stay is sought) is restricted solely to said Wanamaker's dealings in the so-called "Structo" toy product, said to be manufactured by the Structo Manufacturing Company, of Freeport, Illinois.

II.

The present proceeding involves a question now pending before this Court for its decision in the aforesaid certiorari proceedings in the earlier companion First Suit, to wit:

> *Does the issue of said First Suit embrace said Wanamaker's dealings in both the aforesaid American Model Builder and Structo products?*

In its decision in said First Suit, the Respondent Court of Appeals has adjudged that question in the negative (250 Fed., 250, 252). If that is correct, then this Second Suit is superfluous and should not be merely stayed but discontinued or dismissed.

But, until this Court renders its decision on said question, uncertainty exists as to the relationship of the two suits and the proper procedure to be followed therein. Hence, this Second Suit should be stayed until this Court renders its said decision, which, in its disposition of the question of the scope of the issue of the First Suit, will control the future course of both causes.

III.

In conflict with its own decision (250 Fed., 250) in the First Wanamaker Suit (that the issue of said suit embraces the issue of this Second Wanamaker Suit), the Respondent Court of Appeals, as heretofore stated, has not only refused to stay this Second Suit, but has refused to disturb the aforesaid order of the Respondent District Court setting the same down peremptorily for trial. In other words, in denying Petitioner certain relief in the First Wanamaker Suit, the Respondent Court of Appeals based its denial upon a finding (250 Fed., 252) that the issue of said suit embraces the acts of Wanamaker constituting the more specific issue of this Second Suit. In refusing to stay this Second Suit, the action of said Respondent Court of Appeals is directly inconsistent and in conflict with its said decision that the issue of this Second Suit *is* embraced by the First Suit.

IV.

Your Petitioner submits the following as the main

QUESTIONS PRESENTED

(a) Whether the Respondent Courts, or either of them, may disregard the pendency before this Court of the companion First Suit between the same parties, presenting for decision the precise question here involved (which decision will be controlling in this Second Suit sought to be stayed), and proceed with trial of this Second Suit without awaiting decision of this Court in said First Case.

(b) More specifically, may the Respondent Courts, or either of them, disregard the fact that the precise question, upon the basis of which stay is asked—to wit, whether the issue of the First Wanamaker Suit is generic (embracing

Wanamaker's dealings in both the American Model Builder and Structo products), or is specific (embracing only Wanamaker's dealings in the American Model Builder product) —is now before this Court for its decision in said certiorari proceedings (No. 614, October Term, 1918) in the First Wanamaker Suit.

(c) Whether the Respondent Courts may compel a trial of this Second Wanamaker Suit regardless of the fact that said Respondent Court of Appeals has itself decided that the First Wanamaker Suit embraces the issue of this Second Suit; and which decision, unless and until reversed by this Court in said certiorari proceedings, renders it wholly unnecessary to burden the Courts and the parties with the work and heavy expense of trial or other proceedings in this Second Suit—renders wholly unnecessary two trials of the two suits—and, in operation and effect, bars the Second Suit.

(d) Whether or not the Respondent Court of Appeals erred in not overruling the Respondent District Court's aforesaid order of Feb. 6th, 1919, refusing stay, etc.—and in dismissing Petitioner's appeal (taken from said order under Section 129 of the Judicial Code)—and in dismissing the Petition for Mandamus, etc., which sought a review of said order.

Further, and more specifically, your petitioner shows:

V.

The aforesaid two Wanamaker Suits were preceded by the aforesaid Wagner Ohio Suit, wherein, after trial (at which the defendant Wagner testified at length) and final hearing, the District Court (Judge HOLLISTER, 234

Fed., 912) and the Court of Appeals for the Sixth Circuit (246 Fed., 603—reaffirmed in 246 Fed., 610) adjudged that the Ohio defendants, Wagner et al., had been guilty of unfair competition by manufacturing and selling a structural toy known as "American Model Builder," and granted a perpetual injunction. Said Ohio suit and said First Wanamaker Suit both originally charged not only (1) "unfair competition," but also (2) copyright infringement, and also (3) infringement of a certain Hornby Patent. But said patent, having been held invalid by the C. C. A. for the Sixth Circuit, the charge of patent infringement has been dismissed from said Wagner Ohio Suit and has been withdrawn from said First Wanamaker Suit (see statement at top of p. 251 of 250 Fed. Rep.). This Second Wanamaker Suit charges "unfair competition" *alone*.

VI.

Notwithstanding the aforesaid decision of Judge HOLLISTER, and a decree of July 8, 1916, entered thereon against the manufacturer Wagner and his co-defendant in said Ohio Suit, and notwithstanding further warnings given said John Wanamaker, New York, upon the basis of said decision and decree, said Wanamaker continued to offer for sale, and to sell, the American Model Builder product procured by it from said Wagner. Thereupon, on or about Dec. 14, 1916, Petitioner instituted the First Wanamaker Suit; a preliminary injunction was granted by Judge A. N. HAND (241 Fed., 133); and the writ of injunction was issued and served about Jan. 24, 1917. Said defendant then appealed from said injunction-order; and two decisions were thereafter rendered by the Respondent Court of Appeals (250 Fed., 250; Id. 450, 453).

VII.

While under preliminary injunction in the First Wanamaker Suit, the aforesaid John Wanamaker, New York, extensively offered for sale and sold another structural toy product known as "Structo" (alleged to be procured by said Wanamaker from a concern known as the Structo Mfg. Co.—see paragraph XV of Bill of Complaint. Thereupon, on January 22nd, 1918, and prior to the Respondent Court of Appeals' decisions (as hereinafter set forth) in said First Wanamaker Suit, your Petitioner instituted this Second Wanamaker Suit, charging "unfair competition" *alone*, and involving *solely* said Wanamaker's dealings in said "Structo" product.

VIII.

Following the aforesaid decision of the Court of Appeals for the Sixth Circuit, in the Wagner Ohio suit, Petitioner moved Respondent Court of Appeals, in the First Wanamaker Suit (then pending before said Court on said appeal from Judge A. N. HAND'S said injunction-order), for a decision on the merits therein "upon the ground that the decision * * * of the * * * Court of Appeals for the Sixth Circuit * * * is final and conclusive as to the case at bar (said First Wanamaker Suit) under the principles enunciated by the Supreme Court in the various decisions referred to in the accompanying Brief." Your Petitioner further based said motion upon the showing (by the record then before said Court of Appeals in said First Wanamaker Suit) of identity or privity of parties in interest, and identity of subject-mater and issues, in that suit and the Wagner Ohio Suit.

The Respondent Court of Appeals (Judges ROGERS, LEARNED HAND, and MAYER), in denying Petitioner's said motion in the First Wanamaker Suit, based its decision (250 Fed., 250) upon the adjudged lack of identity of issues in the two suits, holding that the issues were *not* "coextensive," because (italics ours) :

> "It is apparent that some of the issues [in said First Wanamaker Suit] are different from those litigated in Ohio [against Wagner] ; they involve not only the defendant's [John Wanamaker, New York] right to sell Wagner's toys and manuals, but any *others* which it may procure *elsewhere*. We have no right to assume because the defendant allows Wagner to have the chief conduct of the defense, that it has abandoned all rights except that of getting the toys and manuals from him."

In other words, in its said decision, the Respondent Court of Appeals has held that the First Wanamaker Suit in New York involves not only the defendant Wanamaker's right to put out said "American Model Builder" product (supplied by said Ohio defendants, Wagner et al.), but also said Wanamaker's right to put out any *other* structural toys which Wanamaker may procure *elsewhere*—which holding adjudges, of course, that said First Suit involves said Wanamaker's right to put out said "Structo" product (procured from the Structo Co.)—the only product involved in this Second Wanamaker Suit. And it was because the Respondent Court of Appeals thus held that Wanamaker was entitled to its "day in court," *in said First Wanamaker Suit*, upon its right to sell "other" toys, such as "Structo," that said Respondent Court of Appeals denied Petitioner's motion in that suit for a decision on the merits. Having thus been adjudged entitled to enjoy, in the First Wanamaker Suit, its "day in court" on "Structo"—which "day in court" said Wanamaker has been and is now enjoying in said First Wanamaker Suit—Wanamaker is not entitled to still another "day in court" (in this Second Wanamaker Suit also), it being remembered that this Second Wanamaker Suit complains solely of Wanamaker's dealings in said "Structo" product. Said ruling of the Respondent Court of Appeals, therefore, nullifies and bars this Second Wanamaker Suit.

IX.

The aforesaid decision of the Respondent Court of Appeals, that the issue in the First Wanamaker Suit embraces Wanamaker's right to sell "other" toys (such as Structo), which Wanamaker procures *elsewhere* "of others" (such as the Structo Co.), still remains *the law of said New York litigation* between your Petitioner and said Wanamaker; and, until said decision is set aside or modified, it constitutes a bar to the prosecution of this Second Wanamaker Suit, because—

> The *entire subject-matter and issues* in this Second Wanamaker Suit—viz.: Wanamaker's right to put out "Structo" product—*are,* according to said decision, *already embraced in the First Wanamaker Suit;* and the Respondent District Court should not be permitted to conduct a *second* trial (in this later suit) upon issues already presented (and, in effect, precluded) in the earlier suit.

Therefore, so long as said holding of the Respondent Court of Appeals remains the *law of the litigation* between your Petitioner and said Wanamaker, further prosecution of this Second Wanamaker Suit should be *stayed.*

X.

Furthermore, following the rendition by the Respondent Court of Appeals of its said decisions (250 Fed., 250, and

250 Fed., 450) in the First Wanamaker Suit, and upon application of your Petitioner, this Court, on or about October 28th, 1918, *granted* its Writ of Certiorari for review of said cause; and said certiorari-proceedings (No. 614, October Term, 1918) are now pending undetermined in this Court. The precise "questions presented" to this Court are set forth on page 4 of said Petition for Certiorari and also in the prayers at the bottom of page 18 and top of page 19. These questions all concern the force and effect to be given, in said First Wanamaker Suit, to the judgment of the Court of Appeals for the Sixth Circuit in the Wagner Ohio Suit; and in particular concern the holding of the Respondent Court of Appeals that the issue in said First Wanamaker Suit embraces, not only Wagner's "The American Model Builder," but other toys which Wanamaker may procure from others (elsewhere) such as "Structo." Thus, the Brief in this Court, in support of the certiorari petition, says:

> "Petitioner seeks a review by this Honorable Court in respect to the failure of the Court of Appeals for the Second Circuit to give proper effect, in this suit, to the judgment of the Court of Appeals for the Sixth Circuit in the earlier Ohio suit." (P. 21 of Brief.)

> "The failure of the Court of Appeals [Second Circuit] to give full force and effect herein to the prior judgment in the Ohio suit *turns upon the sameness of issues in the two suits.* That Court was apparently convinced as to the identity or privity of parties to the two suits." (Brief, page 31.)

Manifestly, therefore, *the question above all others, presented for decision by this Court,* and upon which depends the force and effect to be given the judgment of the Court of Appeals for the Sixth Circuit, *is whether or not the issues in the two suits* (Wagner and First Wanamaker) *are co-extensive.* The pendency of that question before this Court acts as a STAY, not only to proceedings in the First Wanamaker Suit in which the question is directly presented to this Court, but also in this Second Wanamaker Suit, the issues of which (according to the decision of the Respondent Court of Appeals) are embraced in said First Wanamaker Suit.

XI.

Your Petitioner earnestly contends that trial at this time of this Second Wanamaker Suit would not only be *premature,* but would also be *improper*: (a) because in conflict with the present *law* of the litigation (that the issue of the First Wanamaker Suit embraces the "Structo" product) as established by the aforesaid decision of the Respondent Court of Appeals; also (b) because such trial would (in effect) disregard the stay existing in the companion suit (the First Wanamaker Suit) between the same parties, by reason of the pendency of that suit before this Court; (c) because that stay also applies to (and ought to be recognized in) the trial of this Second Wanamaker Suit—the question to be decided by this Court (the scope of the issue in the First Wanamaker Suit) being determinative of whether or not this Second Wanamaker Suit has any reason for existence, and hence whether there will be necessity for any independent trial thereof; and (d) because the decision of this Court in the First Wanamaker Suit will also be controlling as to whether or not the judgment of the courts of the Sixth Circuit in the Wagner Ohio Suit constitutes estoppel by judgment, or is *res adjudicata,* as applied (not only to the First Wanamaker Suit, but also) to this Second Wanamaker Suit.

XII.

And now your Petitioner shows that it has made application to the Respondent District Court to postpone the trial of this Second Wanamaker Suit, in order to await this Court's decision upon said certiorari proceedings in the First Wanamaker Suit. But said District Court has *refused* to postpone, and has, by its order aforesaid, peremptorily set this Second Wanamaker Suit down for trial during the then-ensuing March Term of 1919. And, no equity session of said Court having been held during the month of March, 1919, said order approved and affirmed by the Respondent Court of Appeals, as presently shown, still stands in full force and effect, and requires this cause to be heard at the next ensuing session of said District Court, which your Petitioner is now informed, is to begin May 5th, 1919, with this Second Wanamaker Suit number thirteen on the list.

XIII.

Your Petitioner further shows that it duly brought said order of the Respondent District Court, of Feb. 6, 1919, before the Respondent Court of Appeals for review, by means of appeal. Thereupon said defendant-appellee, Wanamaker, moved to dismiss said appeal on the alleged ground that said Court of Appeals had no jurisdiction to entertain the same. At the conclusion of oral arguments by counsel for both parties, said Court of Appeals (Judges ROGERS and HOUGH), on April 7th, 1919, granted said motion from the bench and dismissed said appeal, and on April 17th, 1919, entered its hereinbefore quoted order of dismissal.

XIV.

Your Petitioner further shows that, on April 7th, 1919 (at the conclusion of the aforesaid arguments on the motion to dismiss), it presented before said Respondent Court of Appeals a Petition for Writ of Mandamus, or, for Writ of Prohibition, or, for Writ of Certiorari, praying said Court of Appeals, for reasons such as set forth in the present petition, to stay the trial and other proceedings in this Second Wanamaker Suit. But thereupon said Court of Appeals (Judges ROGERS and HOUGH), merely upon the basis of a brief oral statement by counsel for Petitioner of the purport of said petition, announced from the bench its decision dismissing said petition, and has entered its hereinbefore quoted order of April 17th, 1919, denying said petition.

XV.

Your Petitioner further shows that it has served upon counsel for the defendant, John Wanamaker, New York, in said Second Wanamaker Suit (in which stay is sought) its petition to this Court for a writ of certiorari to the Court of Appeals for the Second Circuit said petition being noticed for submission to this Court on Monday, May 12th, 1919. But because of unavoidable delay in procuring a transcript of record, and printing the same, and further because of adjournment of this Court (as your Petitioner is informed) over May 12th, 1919, until Monday, May 19th, 1919, it will be impossible to submit said petition prior to the date last named. Wherefore, and in view of the exigencies of the situation, and the probability that said Second Wanamaker Suit may be reached for trial in the Respondent District Court before said petition for writ of certiorari can be submitted to this Court, your Petitioner seeks relief and a stay of said trial by the present petition for writ of mandamus, or, in the alternative, for writ of prohibition.

WHEREFORE, and being without other relief to stay the trial and other proceedings in this Second Wanamaker Suit, pending the decision of this Honorable Court in said First Wanamaker Suit, your Petitioner prays as follows:

(1) That this Honorable Court will either *postpone* the trial of your Petitioner's said Second Wanamaker Suit, and *stay* all proceedings therein, until this Court renders its decision upon said certiorari proceedings arising out of said First Wanamaker Suit; or will direct and instruct the respondent courts to do so.

(2) Or, in the alternative, that the writ of mandamus, or, in the alternative, the writ of prohibition, may issue out of this Court directed to the respondent Circuit Court of Appeals for the Second Circuit, and the judges thereof, and to the respondent District Court for the Southern District of New York, and the judges thereof, requiring said courts to postpone trial of and suspend proceedings in said Second Wanamaker Suit as aforesaid.

(3) That this Honorable Court will enter and issue a rule requiring said respondent courts, and the judges thereof, to show cause why the writ of mandamus, or, in the alternative, the writ of prohibition, should not issue against them.

(4) And that this Court will make such other and further directions, and grant such other and further relief, as equity and good practice may require.

And your Petitioner will ever pray.

MECCANO, LIMITED,

By: REEVE LEWIS,

C. A. L. MASSIE,

W. B. KERKAM,

RALPH L. SCOTT,

Of Counsel.

Washington, D. C.,
    May 1st, 1919.

District of Columbia, *ss*:

Reeve Lewis, being duly sworn, deposes and says, he is of counsel for Meccano Limited in the hereinbefore named suits in New York and in Ohio; that he has read the foregoing petition and knows the contents thereof; and that he believes the same to be true.

REEVE LEWIS.

Subscribed and sworn to before me this 1st day of May, 1919:

J. E. NELL,
Notary Public.

BRIEF IN SUPPORT OF PETITION.

Following the not uncommon practice exemplified in
In Re SIMONS, 247 U. S. 231; 62 Law. Ed. 1094; 38 S.
C. R. 497, Petitioher asks "for mandamus, or, if that is denied, for prohibition or certiorari"; and, as stated in said
decision, "it does not matter very much in what form an
extraordinary remedy is afforded in this case."

One of two antithetical and contradictory propositions
must be true: That is—

Either (1): All the issues involved in this Second Wanamaker Suit are *already presented* in the First Wanamaker
Suit;

Or (2): This Second Suit contains one or more issues
not presented in that First Suit.

Of these two propositions (the only two alternatives),
one or the other *must* be correct, and the remaining one in-
correct. No other situation is possible.

The Respondent Court of Appeals, in its opinion of
March, 1918 (250 Fed. 250, denying Petitioner's motion
for interlocutory decree in the First Wanamaker Suit), has
asserted and upheld the first-named proposition, as ma-
terial and controlling.

As between the two aforesaid diametrically opposite
views (and there is no third view possible), the one laid
down by the Respondent Court of Appeals *must prevail,*
whether right or wrong, until it is authoritatively changed
or modified by this Court. Having intervened in said First
Wanamaker Suit by its writ of certiorari, it now rests with
this Court alone to change or modify said ruling that the
issues of the First Wanamaker Suit embrace said Wanamaker's dealings in "Structo," the sole issue of the Second
Wanamaker Suit. That ruling cannot be accepted as correct for *one* purpose (viz.: the Respondent Court of Ap-

peals' denial of our motion for interlocutory decree, 250 Fed. 250), and the opposite and conflicting view accepted as correct for *another* purpose (viz.: denying our motion for suspension of trial of this Second Wanamaker Suit). There should be no shifting from one view to the other; yet that is the effect of the refusal of the Respondent Courts to suspend trial of this Second Wanamaker Suit.

Upon the facts and circumstances asserted in the petition, the trial and other proceedings in this Second Wanamaker Suit should be suspended and postponed for the following reasons:

I. THE HOLDING OF THE RESPONDENT COURT OF APPEALS THAT THE SUBJECT-MATTER AND ISSUES OF THE FIRST WANAMAKER SUIT COMPRISE THE ENTIRE SUBJECT-MATTER AND ISSUES OF THIS SECOND WANAMAKER SUIT.

The *reason* assigned by the Respondent Court of Appeals in its decision (250 Fed. 250) denying Petitioner's motion for decision on the merits in the First Wanamaker Suit, was because of the unanimous opinion of that Court (p. 252) that:

> "It is apparent that some of the issues [in said earlier Wanamaker Suit] are different from those litigated in Ohio; they [the issues in said First Wanamaker Suit] involve, not only the defendant's [Wanamaker's] right to sell Wagner's [Ohio] toys and manuals, but *any* others which it [Wanamaker] may procure *elsewhere*. We have no right to assume * * * that it [Wanamaker] has abandoned all rights, except that of getting the toys and manuals from him [Wagner]."

Said Court was right in its conjecture, since it now appears that said Wanamaker *is* handling "other" structural

toys, viz.: the Structo product, said to be procured from the
Structo Mfg. Co. The Structo toys specifically complained
of in this Second Wanamaker Suit, are clearly among the
"others" which said Court refers to. Judge LEARNED
HAND'S subsequent *dissenting* opinion (250 Fed. 453)
repeats:

> "Of course, as we held in the earlier case [250 Fed.
> 450, supra], Wanamaker must have its day in court
> upon its own right to make and sell the toys or to buy
> them of *others*."

That is to say: The Judges of Respondent Court of Appeals have concurred in holding that said First Wanamaker
Suit not only involves the Wagner Ohio product, but also
involves the *Structo* product. And this issue—whether or
not Wanamaker has the right to procure "Structo" toys
(from the Structo Mfg. Co.) and sell them to others, without violating any of Petitioner's rights—is the *sole* issue
presented in this Second Wanamaker Suit.

It being thus established, by the decision of the Respondent Court of Appeals, that the First Wanamaker Suit embraces the sole issue of this Second Wanamaker Suit, *that*
holding stands as the law of this litigation between Meccano and Wanamaker, and so remains until said decision
is set aside or modified by this Court. Such *law of the litigation,* so long as it stands, not only renders this Second
Wanamaker Suit superfluous, but constitutes a *bar* thereto,
and supersedes all discretion, or authority, of the Respondent Courts to take any action in this Second Wanamaker
Suit in conflict with said law, and particularly to proceed
with trial of this Second Suit. And, if the matter be in
any way open to discretion, it is an improvident exercise of,
and abuse of, such discretion to try this Second Wanamaker

Suit, or to assign it for trial under the circumstances aforesaid.

II. THE PENDENCY BEFORE THIS COURT, FOR ITS DETERMINATION IN THE FIRST WANAMAKER SUIT, OF THE QUESTION WHETHER OR NOT THAT SUIT ALSO EMBRACES THE SOLE ISSUE OF THIS SECOND WANAMAKER SUIT, HAS THE EFFECT OF STAYING TRIAL OF THIS SECOND SUIT.

The mere granting of this Court's writ of certiorari in the First Wanamaker Suit operates *ipso facto* to STAY, in the Respondent Courts, all further proceedings in that suit. Thus, the Court of Appeals for the Ninth Circuit has said, through Circuit Judge GILBERT (emphasis is ours):

> "A certiorari to a subordinate court or tribunal operates as a stay of proceedings *from the time of its service or of formal notice of its issuance,* and if the court to which the writ is directed thereafter proceeds, it is a contempt, and its subsequent proceedings are *void.* 6 Cyc. 800, and cases there cited. The proceedings of this court are not reversed by the issuance of the writ and the stay resulting therefrom, but are merely *suspended* until the further action of the reviewing court. Ewing vs. Thompson, 43 Pa. 372."
>
> Waskey vs. Hammer; 179 Fed. 273,274.

As the particular question to be decided by this Court in the First Wanamaker Suit, to wit—whether the issue thereof embraces toys such as "Structo"—will be determinative of the reason for the existence of this Second Wanamaker Suit (the issue of which is confined to said Structo toy), we respectfully insist that the pendency of that question before this Court, in said companion suit between the same parties, and under the existing circumstances, operates *ipso facto* to also stay further proceedings in this Second Wanamaker Suit. At the very least, the pendency of said certiorari proceedings before this Court *ought* to be regarded, out of the respect due this Court, as constituting (in effect) a stay of all proceedings in this Second Wanamaker Suit between the same parties, in the *same* District Court, and involving the *same* question. Yet, both Respondent Courts have refused to stay, and the Respondent District Court has peremptorily set this Second Wanamaker Suit down for trial at an early date.

Wherefore, we earnestly and confidently urge this Court to grant the relief now prayed for; and to stay the trial and all further proceedings in this Second Wanamaker Suit, or to direct the Respondent Courts to stay, until the rendition of this Court's forthcoming decision in said certiorari proceedings (No. 614, October Term, 1918) in the First Wanamaker Suit.

Respectfully submitted,

MECCANO LIMITED,

By REEVE LEWIS,

C. A. L. MASSIE,

W. B. KERKAM,

RALPH L. SCOTT,

Of Counsel for Petitioner.

Washington, D. C., May 1, 1919.

Lightning Source UK Ltd.
Milton Keynes UK
UKOW05f1025191117
312967UK00006B/152/P